Reiki
a manual

Maia Kumari Gilman

ASEI ARTS, A DIVISION OF LIGHT VIBE LLC
NEW YORK

Copyright ©2019 Maia Kumari Gilman

All rights reserved. No part of this book may be used or reproduced in any manner whatsoever without written permission from the publisher except in the case of brief quotations embodied in critical articles or reviews. For information, contact: ASEI Arts, a division of Light Vibe LLC, 112 West 27th Street, Suite 500, New York NY 10001, email: admin@aseiarts.com

Published by ASEI Arts, a division of Light Vibe LLC, New York NY

Distributed by Ingram

Name: Gilman, Maia Kumari, author

Title: Reiki: a manual / Maia Kumari Gilman

Description: Third US edition | New York NY: ASEI Arts, a division of Light Vibe LLC, 2019

Identifiers: ISBN 13: 978-0-9988421-4-1

Third US edition 2019

Design Advisor: Lori Dalvi

www.aseiarts.com

To my beloved earth

Contents

The Reiki Ideals	9
New Foreword	11
Can I learn Reiki by reading this book?	15
What is Reiki?	1
What is Reiki not?	3
What does Reiki do?	7
What does Reiki feel like?	9
Who can practice Reiki?	11

Where can Reiki be practiced?	13
Who benefits from Reiki?	15
What is the goal of Reiki?	17
What is the history of Reiki?	21
Reiki and the human energy body	27
Preparing yourself for a Reiki attunement	33
Preparing for a Reiki session	37
Conducting a Reiki session	41
Finishing a Reiki session	45
Using Reiki with children and in parenting	49
Using Reiki in studying, career development and in the workplace	55
Connecting harmonic sound with Reiki	61
Setting up your Reiki practice	67
Continuing studies in Reiki	71
Using symbols: a higher level of study	75

A Reiki blessing by Mildred   79
McCaine, in closing

Resources about Reiki   81

The Reiki Ideals

The secret art of inviting happiness
The miraculous medicine of all diseases
Just for today, do not anger
Do not worry and be filled with gratitude
Devote yourself to your work. Be kind to
people. Every morning and evening, join
your hands in prayer.
Pray these words to your heart
and chant these words with your mouth

Usui Reiki Treatment for the
improvement of body and mind

—The founder, Usui Mikao

This training manual is for use in Usui Reiki workshops. We do not diagnose or treat specific illnesses and recommend that you seek the assistance of a medical doctor if you are unwell. Reiki is not a replacement for medical care.

Reiki is for relaxation and wellness.

New Foreword

It is eleven years since I first wrote and used this teaching manual and in that time, I have changed and so has my approach to Reiki. I am much more likely to use the word "allowing" in place of "Reiki," which I find makes the practice less esoteric and much more accessible to any and everyone. It takes away the mystery and puts the power in the hands of the people—where it belongs.

I have also not been teaching Reiki for some time, which has given me a stepped-back perspective on the tradition and many of its distinctions. I run Reiki every day in my own life and work, and it's a beautiful flow—a beautiful allowing. It opens doors. And it's not so unique—many do this in varied traditions around the world, each with a different name. It's all the same thing in my eyes: being open to the flow of energy.

This book excludes one chapter of the original manual, entitled "Space Clearing Using Level 1 Reiki." This is for two reasons:

1. the chapter was published as a standalone article by the International Association of Reiki Professionals' *Reiki Times*, and
2. my feelings, understanding and intuition around the idea of space clearing are evolving.

I am working on a separate book on the topic of raising the subtle energy of spaces, and this book will integrate the work I have carried out in architecture, concurrent with my development of products in aromatherapy for homes, within Light Vibe LLC.

This book excludes any diagrams about hand-scanning and any class handouts about Reiki. This is intentional, as it is assumed that the teacher who uses this book in class will have handouts from their own tradition of teaching. It is also a way of paying respect to some of the more private traditions within Reiki, such as the one-to-one sharing of Reiki symbols between teacher and students.

This book is intended to be appreciated by anyone, regardless of their background in Reiki. For that reason, I have eliminated traditional references to "levels" in Reiki until the end.

I continue to love and practice Reiki, and am now integrating Reiki into my fiction writing, as evidenced in my novel *The Erenwine Agenda*, a new frontier for me that I'm enjoying very much. What matters to me these days is the journey to that new frontier, much more so than the labels we put on how we get there.

—Maia Kumari Gilman,
Reiki Master Teacher and Registered Architect

Can I learn Reiki by reading this book?

In a word: no. You can learn about *my perspective on Reiki* by reading this book. By definition, Reiki is a hands-on tradition that is passed from teacher to student. There is debate about whether this can be done long distance over the internet. I wrote a Q&A piece on Quora about this subject which can be viewed here: https://www.quora.com/What-determines-the-power-and-effectiveness-of-a-Reiki-Attunement/answer/Maia-Kumari-Gilman-Architect

The original question asked on Quora was:

What determines the power and effectiveness of a Reiki Attunement? I ask this question in the context of concerns (e.g. within the UK Reiki Federation) over allowing distance attunements for training professional Reiki practitioners.

My answer on Quora is:

I am a Reiki Master Teacher in the US and will answer based on my experience here, and with your larger context in mind.

In general, I would say the power of a Reiki attunement comes from:

- *the readiness and openness of the recipient;*
- *the clarity, intention and preparedness of the giver;*

- and the presetting of the environment to be conducive to a positive flow.

Specifically, as I was taught, the Reiki attunement as a "thing" gains its power from being a Reiki Attunement Ceremony. And those ceremonial aspects, while possible in a distant fashion, are more powerful, in my experience, by proximity. Being there is different. Is it better? I think it may be the better choice for one who does not have the option of attending in person.

I find, personally, that there is a thinness, a flimsiness to the feeling I get from the online Reiki attunements I am aware of. That could be because of:

- where I was at personally when I glanced at them;
- the energy around the intentions of the person who created the online program;
- and my perception of that person's intentions at the time.

To take an analysis further would, I think, be using our energy-senses to foster or bolster a personal agenda...It sounds like there is an agenda – is that too strong a word in this case? – in the UK situation with distant attunements. I presume these distant attunements occur within the context of online courses.

From what I sense, it is the online aspect that can distort, dilute or distract the experience, and it is not the distant Reiki itself. Reiki is a powerful tool (and in the framework of broader energy work, we could call Reiki "allowing") and it is through this Allowing or Reiki to flow, that we bolster our larger well-being. Distant Reiki is, in my experience, incredibly powerful as a tool to enable an expanded Allowing, and by extension so would be a distant attunement.

I think we would do well to learn how to manage the merging vibrations of internet and Reiki to form a consistent practice – likely, it is the way of the future.

I include myself in this group who need to consider a balance between merging technological/subtle vibrations while also "decluttering" our energy spheres.

A topic for a future novel, to be sure. Thank you for the excellent and thought-provoking question! (I'm going to take some notes for my next book now...!)

Sending you Reiki blessings from the US,

-Maia

1

What is Reiki?

Reiki is a learned system of hands-on healing in which the practitioner channels clear energy to the client for the client's own well-being. Hands-on healing is a time-honored practice that exists in many cultures around the world. The word Reiki comes from the Japanese "rei" which means "universal life force" and "ki" or "chi" which means "life flow"[1]. Through deep meditation, Reiki's founder Mikao Usui tapped into this practice.

Many scholars of Reiki have delved into its history and this can be understood in greater depth by reading a variety of sources that are listed in the Resources section at the end of this manual. Those most valuable sources are the ones that have traced the journey and development of Reiki back to Japan.

[1] Definition of Reiki (Rand, 2000)

2

What is Reiki not?

Reiki is not a religious practice and it does not appear to have its roots in a particular religion. People of all religious and cultural backgrounds practice Reiki and benefit from its healing effects.

At present there is a dialogue in the Catholic Church in the United States about the history of Reiki and its place in the Church. The Catholic

Church has released a statement saying that since Reiki cannot be traced definitively to either Christian or scientific roots, it is not supported by the Church[1]. This is a matter of personal preference; many Christian and Catholic Reiki practitioners exist, and come to their own decisions about how to integrate their beliefs with those of the Church.

Reiki is accepted by many hospitals (in stress reduction to patients before and after surgery[2]), cancer clinics (in providing relaxation and pain management to patients[3]) and the US military (in treatment of soldiers with Post Traumatic Stress Disorder[4]). Some nursing schools teach another version of hands-on healing called Therapeutic Touch and its essence is similar to that of Reiki[5]. Reiki continues to benefit a huge cross-section of our society, outside of the views of religious institutions.

[1] Reiki and the Catholic Church (Butt, 2009)

[2] Reiki used with surgery (NIH, 2008)

[3] Reiki in cancer clinics (American Cancer Society, 2008)

[4] Use of Reiki in military's treatment of PTSD (US Veterans Affairs, 2009)

[5] Teaching of Therapeutic Touch in schools of nursing (Beth Israel Hospital CCHH, 2008)

3

What does Reiki do?

I believe that all who practice Reiki would agree on one thing: it helps the client to relax[1]. Once the body is in a relaxed state, it can get to work on healing itself and returning to a state of balance[2]. Some Reiki practitioners add that Reiki can remove energetic blockages that may lead to disease[3]. In order to balance the range of opinion in the Reiki and medical worlds in this teaching manual, I take the position that Reiki is for relaxation, and that any other health benefits that occur are welcome, although not assured or quantifiable.

[1] Reiki for relaxation (Fernandez, 2004)

[2] Healing and relaxation (Dale, 2009)

[3] Energetic blockages and disease (Adam, 2007)

4

What does Reiki feel like?

To clients or recipients, Reiki may feel like warm heat, cool sensations, energized tingling, rolling waves or moving streams. Clients may have sensory or extra-sensory perceptions including an awareness of the movement of light and color and visions or visualizations related to their own healing or releasing of past experiences. Some clients fall asleep during a session.

To practitioners, Reiki may feel like warmth coming through their hands, head or feet, or those parts may feel very cold. Sometimes practitioners will feel that their hands are ice cold while the clients they are working with experience simultaneously that the practitioners' hands are very warm. At times, clients will feel that the practitioners' hands are moving when in fact they are still, or that the practitioners' hands are over one part of the clients' body when in fact they are over another[1].

[1] Practitioners' and clients' personal communication with Maia Gilman

Who can practice Reiki?

Reiki is a learned art form, so anyone can become a practitioner. Some people may have a head start in energy work due to their own innate inclinations toward healing. Everyone who is attuned to Reiki will benefit from its healing effects in their own lives, if they continue to practice. Some people who are drawn to the healing arts are in need of personal healing themselves, and practicing Reiki is part of their own journey. Some who practice Reiki do so out of a genuine desire to assist others in reaching their deeper human potential. Others come to Reiki out of curiosity to learn something new.

There is no correct path to Reiki. Everyone who practices Reiki stands to benefit, regardless of their initial motivations for pursuing its study.

6

Where can Reiki be practiced?

While Reiki is often practiced in a studio or clinic setting on a massage or Reiki table, it can actually be practiced anywhere, and across any distance. The client remains comfortably clothed and either seated or lying down. The practitioner moves his or her hands around the client—either with hands on or hands slightly above the body—in a series of motions that are in part learned and yet also intuitively guided. The clear energy of Reiki comes through the practitioner to the client, and moves through the client to wherever in the body it is most needed.

This can also be done across a distance—in the next room, or across to the next continent. It is through the power of the practitioner's intention and visualization that the target of distant Reiki is met. We will talk in greater detail about distant Reiki as we progress through the class material, with attention to real world examples where it has had a beneficial effect.

7

Who benefits from Reiki?

Anyone can benefit from Reiki; it will be more beneficial to you if you are open to receiving from others. If you are in a particularly closed-minded state, or feeling shut off from others, it may take longer for the Reiki to affect you in a positive way[1]. Reiki is not just for those in need of assistance in dealing with a major illness, but for everyone, regardless of your state of health or state of mind. It is helpful to use Reiki with children who are having a hard time settling down. Reiki can be used with pets, plants, houses—you name it. You do not need to have a particular view or opinion of the universe or consciousness in order to see and experience that all things can benefit from an infusion of Reiki energy.

1] Practitioners' observations shared with Maia Gilman

8

What is the goal of Reiki?

We are not attempting to "cure" with Reiki. We are bringing "healing" or "wholeness" to the person's body, mind and spirit through Reiki. By bringing the body, mind and spirit into balance, your clients—who could include you—have a stronger and clearer base from which to move forward.[1]

By following the hand positions outlined in the pages ahead, you will find that you can bring healing to yourself and to your clients quite effectively. The hand positions are traditional Reiki forms, but with every teacher after Usui, the hand positions have been taught slightly differently. You will notice minor changes within each lineage. This is a normal evolutionary process and is acceptable in Reiki.

By using your intuition in placing your hands in Reiki, you will tap into the greatest potential in your ability to assist others in their healing. By learning to trust your intuition and to test it out with clients, you will amaze and surprise yourself with the energized results. This is a time-honored part of Reiki, and one that asks you to look inward to your own stillness for guidance.

[1] Definitions of curing, healing and wellness (Dale, 2009)

9

What is the history of Reiki?

Reiki was developed by Mikao Usui in the early 1900s in Japan. He was a Buddhist scholar who studied ancient Tibetan Buddhist texts, meditated and synthesized the wisdom of Reiki while in a deep meditative state. Some Reiki scholars believe he read about the healing practice in the texts, while others believe he received them directly in an enlightened state.[1]

After careful consideration, Usui shared his experiences with others close to him and began to teach Reiki. He is thought to have attuned 20 students to the tradition. In 1923 there was a devastating earthquake in and around Tokyo, where Usui had set up a clinic. Usui immediately put himself and his students to work in assisting the local population by offering Reiki. The popularity of Reiki spread after this, and Usui received honors from the Emperor of Japan for his work.

Usui initially attuned three masters into the Reiki tradition. One of his students, Chijiro Hayashi, was a naval officer who sought to bring Reiki to greater prominence. Hayashi treated a cancer patient called Hawayo Takata, and in turn, Takata became attuned as a Reiki Master herself. Mrs. Takata began to teach Reiki in Hawaii where she was born. This represents the introduction of Reiki to the West, and the origin of the branch of Reiki most commonly practiced in North America.[2]

An inscribed memorial stone in Japan gives a posthumous description of Usui himself, and the development of Reiki. Mrs. Takata declared that Usui was Christian, although there is no evidence of this in the memorial inscription in Japan. She may have been attempting to blend Usui and Reiki into a predominantly Christian post-WW II environment in the US, making adjustments as she saw fit.[3]

Every teacher of Reiki has influenced the practice with their own intuitive guidance and wisdom. If you trace your lineage back, you will find that all paths lead to Usui. If they do not, then you are not practicing Usui

Reiki, but another form of intuitive healing. Many people who study Reiki can trace several lineages with different teachers. My own work in Reiki comes through two lineages.

Mikao Usui →

Chijiro Hayashi →

Hawayo Takata →

Iris Ishikura →

Arthur Roberston →

Michael Alatriste →

Bonnie Berke →

Amy Leban Witmyer →

Maia Kumari Gilman

and

Mikao Usui →

Chijiro Hayashi →

Hawayo Takata →

Barbara Ray →

Judy Seeley →

Karen Patton →

Kathie Lipinski →

Jennifer Staib →

Maia Kumari Gilman

[1] Development of Reiki (Ellyard, 2006)

[2] Spread of Reiki to the West (Ellyard, 2006)

[3] Takata's influence (Ellyard, 2006)

10

Reiki and the human energy body

Reiki healing works with energy in and beyond the human body. In some traditions, the body is thought to be driven by energetic centers which operate like batteries in the body. These are known as chakras in the East, and there may be as few as four or as many as twelve chakras observed. In the most popular understanding of the chakra system in the West, there are seven chakras. These are aligned along the head, neck and spine and project outward.[1]

As you practice Reiki, you may notice that your hands are drawn to these different energy centers and that you have an expanding awareness of their effects. You can send Reiki to the chakras, visualizing their pure colors as you do. This is a very soothing way to practice Reiki on yourself, too, as it helps you to rebalance.

There are the seven basic chakras and their characteristics listed here, as most often described in Western Reiki. This is an evolving system, both in terms of its understanding and also in our subtle-body experience, in that both understanding and experience are always expanding. It's not recommended to be too attached to this system; it is shared here for larger context. The seven traditional Western-described chakras are:

first chakra · location: groin · color: red · sound: *lam* or "lahmng" · expression: trust

second chakra · location: abdomen · color: orange · sound: *vam* or "vahmng" · expression: sexuality

third chakra · location: navel · color: yellow · sound: *ram* or "rahmng" · expression: confidence

fourth chakra · location: heart · color: green · sound: *yam* or "yahmng" · expression: respect

fifth chakra · location: throat · color: · blue · sound: *ham* or "hahmng" · expression: communication

sixth chakra · location: forehead ·

color: indigo · sound: *om, aum* or "*auhmng*"· expression: self-awareness

seventh chakra · location: top of head · color: violet · sound: *ng* or "ngh" · expression: wisdom[2]

When you work with the energy of the body in Reiki, you not only connect with the chakras. You also touch and heal the aura. My experience of the aura is that it is composed of onion-like energetic rings around and through the human body. Some systems of understanding connect the auric layers to the chakras and to the meridians or rivers of energy that run through the body.

Step outside these descriptive systems for a moment and try this to develop your understanding of the aura. This is a fun exercise but is not required in a practice of Reiki.

Use your hand to feel the energy

outside of your body. It extends in layers, and with practice you can feel and see these layers.

Try standing in front of a mirror with an even light and a neutral colored background.

Let your eyes go softly out of focus and look at your shoulder in the mirror.

You may see a faint or bright corona of light around you.

Do this every day until you are able to hold the vision of the aura steady.

When you work with Reiki clients, look for and feel this aura, too.

You can incorporate your awareness of the aura into your practice but there is no need to get overly analytical about it or what its color or condition means as it is ever-changing.

Simply observe it and notice where your hands are drawn to be in your Reiki practice.

Areas of the aura that look or feel weak or distressed will benefit from your Reiki hands.

Imagine the imbalances as perfectly restored, perfectly balanced.

Your job is not to diagnose or to manage this information. Your ability is to bring someone—including yourself—comfort by the placement of your hands, by the presence of your human connection, and by your clarity and openness to bringing Reiki energy through you for that person's own benefit.

[1] Chakra systems (Dale, 2009)

[2] Yoga sounds per Ruth Cunningham

11

Preparing yourself for a Reiki attunement

Receiving a Reiki attunement is like having a Reiki session, only more intense, and with the purpose of "passing the torch" so that you, too, can channel Reiki energy to others. In an attunement you receive an energetic adjustment that is a bit like tuning a radio to a clear signal.

There are a few things that are helpful to do in the days before your Reiki attunement. These are in no particular order, and all are optional although suggested.

Eat a clean diet free of pesticides and added hormones.

Eat a diet low in meat and dairy (you don't have to become vegetarian if you are not already!).

Keep up your intake of water, six to eight glasses per day.

Reduce alcohol and recreational drugs.

Reduce your caffeine intake (don't make yourself crazy so if you need that one cup to get you started in the morning, be realistic with yourself).

The dietary notes above tend to

increase your personal wellbeing and raise your energy which helps in your experience of receiving the Reiki attunement.

Get adequate sleep when you are tired. For some people this might be six hours, for others ten. Be the best judge of your needs, and prioritize them.

Keep a journal about thoughts, sensations and experiences that you are having and that you would like to see change. This is a powerful tool and we'll use it during the workshop. It will remain confidential, just between you and the pages.

Don't worry too much about reading up on Reiki before the class, unless you are particularly drawn to do so. You will receive history and theory information in class, plus recommended reading for after the attunement. It is best to experience

Reiki fully in your body, before you try to pull book learning into your understanding. The information you read in books will be a good supplement to your knowledge after the Reiki class, rather than before. Reiki really cannot be learned or experienced from a book or video, although the resources are helpful in building your practice later.

12

Preparing for a Reiki session

Turn off cell phones entirely, rather than leave them on a "vibrate" setting. Cell phone waves have been shown to affect the human energy field. If you need to keep your phone on for emergencies, leave it in the next room.

Take a deep breath and feel grounded in the space you are in.

Set your intention to prepare yourself and the room for the Reiki session, and for the incoming client.

Bring the Reiki energy through you and allow it to flow into the room.

Some people like to light candles or use aromatherapy in a Reiki session. Check with your client before you use any scented products, as they may not be to everyone's liking. Even if a client says it is ok, they may become more sensitive during a session so be prepared to put the oils and candles away if you are asked.

Take off any jangly jewelry. Some people think that the metal of jewelry can affect the Reiki transmission. It is important to reduce any disturbances to your client that may come from bracelets, necklaces and earrings making rattling noises. Use your own discretion about this. You can suggest to your client that they remove their jewelry if they want but they do not have to.

You can choose with your client whether or not you will play soft music in the background.

Have a fresh blanket on hand for your client for the session and afterwards in case they feel cold.

Suggest to your client before you begin that they use the restroom, so they do not have to get up in the middle of the session.

Describe to the client the type of experiences and sensations they can expect during and after a session. These may include warmth, tingling, emotional releases, a grumbling stomach and falling asleep. Afterwards, some clients feel these sensations continue and may feel tired. Suggest that they rest and drink water.

Some clients may require more sessions to feel a shift because of more deeply-rooted conditions. Others may respond right away. It all depends on the individual.

Remember, you are not "curing." The goal is to bring the focus back to the wellness that is inherent in everyone. That is the overriding intent of Reiki as I understand it. Keep your focus on the wellness of the individual and not upon their ailment. Your intention is like a laser pointer in its ability to shift the client's own focus to their wellness, and the relaxation that comes with Reiki is the catalyst.

13

Conducting a Reiki session

Prepare yourself and the room as noted on the previous page. It is assumed that a person at this level is familiar with the terms included in this process. Otherwise, seek a local teacher to advise and attune.

Put your hands in *Gassho* or prayer position. Focus on the energy between your two middle fingers where they meet.

Ask the Reiki energy to come through you, and for a specific purpose. Create a saying that you use to bring the Reiki in, such as "Reiki energy, please come through me for I am a clear and open channel, for the best and highest healing good of my client who is here with me now." You can name the client as part of this statement. You can do this in your head or out loud.

Use *Byosen* scanning from head to toe, a few inches off the client's body. Note any sensations in your hands or body and take this as information.

Follow the sequence of hand positions shown in this manual. These are suggested and not required. Keep your hands in place for a few minutes at each position. If your hands feel heavy or hot in a particular location, keep them there longer. You may even stay in one position for an hour.

Follow your intuition about where to go over the body, how to move your hands over the body and how long to stay in different positions. This is as much an intuitively-guided process as it is a learned one. Once you have the Reiki attunement, the Reiki energy will flow when you choose to focus it, even if you don't follow the hand positions.

See the descriptions of the chakra system and harmonic sound for other ideas of how to work with Reiki energy in a session.

Use *Byosen* scanning from head to toe, again a few inches off the body. Note any changes since you first scanned.

End in *Gassho* or prayer position. Create a saying that you will use in closing to seal the healing. You can use language such as "I seal this healing with love and light" or some similar graceful conclusion that is meaningful to you. You can do this out loud or in your head.

Use dry brushing three times down your arms and flick any remaining energy out of the field of you and the client. Imagine the energy being transformed into something positive and passing down the water lines or trees outside, into the earth, for reintegration into the energy of the earth.

14

Finishing a Reiki session

Have your client get off the table or chair and shake out their limbs. This is not a traditional part of Reiki but it is very effective in getting the body changes integrated and reawakening the person who may have become drowsy during the session.

Offer your client a glass of water after the session so that they can continue the process of flushing out toxins that may be released through the Reiki.

Suggest to the client that they take a short walk before driving or engaging with regular activities, to allow time to adjust after the period of deep relaxation.

After your client leaves, send Reiki to the room with the intention of clearing any unhealthy energies that may have been released.

Take a bath in Epsom saltwater, rub with Epsom saltwater, or visualize rubbing with Epsom saltwater, to recharge yourself after a session. You can add some essential oil if it suits you. Lavender is a good one for after a session. Consult with your doctor first.

Allow some time between clients so you can regroup and prepare yourself. It could be fifteen minutes between clients, or a few days before the next session—only you know what feels right for your practice.

15

Using Reiki with children and in parenting

Using Reiki with children is one of the best ways to get immediate hands-on practice. If children already come to you for hugs and kisses when happy, tired, hurt, sleepy, upset, etcetera, you can add Reiki to help them with transitions at the beginning and end of the day, including at bedtime or in the middle of the night.

There is little that is predictable about doing Reiki with small children; it is nothing like being in a calm studio setting. You have to adjust your practice according to their age, temperament, activity level and so on.

Here are some ways you can incorporate Reiki into your parenting routine or your work with children.

Ask a child if he or she would like a warm hand on their hurt, tummy ache, etcetera. Send Reiki through your hands and visualize the hurt dissolving. Ask the child how it feels after a minute or two. You can tell them that you are doing Reiki, which can help hurts go away by using your warm hands. They may ask for this again in the future.

Send a child Reiki at bedtime to help him or her go to sleep. You can incorporate a shielding exercise of pretending to make a camping tent over the bed before going to sleep. Nothing can get in except love, and anything yucky that needs to get out, can get out. No monsters allowed!

Use Reiki with a child who is having a tantrum. You may notice that the tantrum does not subside but actually increases in intensity, comes to a head quickly and then immediately dissipates. The child will likely want a warm snuggle after this. You can continue to use Reiki to settle down.

Sometimes giving a crying child Reiki is not immediately helpful. Try matching your breathing pattern to their breathing pattern if they are in a tantrum. Give them something tactile to hold, a change of scene or temperature, or a cup with a straw to suck on. Once they have begun to calm down a little, then send Reiki.

After a child has been crying in a room, the energy there may be destabilized and uncomfortable for the child, even if they have calmed down. Use Reiki to gently sweep away the residual vibrations of crying and to transform the space quickly into a soothing and safe space once again.

Children love to make noise. Involve your children in rudimentary sound space clearing with drums, bells, singing and the like. While they play, set your intentions to shift out any old energies that may not be serving you well in your home. Imagine the energies dissolving in the sound and being transformed into something positive.

Teach children to be empowered in their dream time. If they have a bad dream, first talk about it to understand its importance, then tell them that they can replace the dream with a better one. Send them back to sleep with a story of a happier scene, and seal the visualization with Reiki.

Use Reiki on yourself, the caregiver, with the intention of smoothing your mood so that you can respond calmly and appropriately to the children you are with. Children mirror our moods so continue to work on your own energy with Reiki, and you will set a positive tone for the children. With children's issues that may not stem from you, you can better respond to their needs if you are coming from a strong and grounded place. Reiki will help you with this.

Some people attune children to Reiki at a young age. I maintain that it is wonderful to practice Reiki on children, but that it is best for them to make their own informed decision as to if and when they wish to become practitioners themselves.

16

Using Reiki in studying, career development and in the workplace

One of the most useful ways to use Reiki outside of the conventional world of health and healing is in your education and work life. Opening yourself to the flow of Reiki energy can sharpen your focus, aid memory retention, identify and eliminate blocks in your progress and help you to achieve goals.

Here are some practical applications of Reiki in your daily work of studying, developing your career and harmonizing your experiences in the work place.

Give Reiki to yourself at your desk, before a meeting, or on a bathroom break. Allow yourself to be fully grounded and present in your work day and let the Reiki energy assist.

Visualize a meeting or interview going well, ahead of time. Send Reiki to the image. If you like, doodle a picture of the meeting or write a description of the scenario, and give Reiki to the picture or passage.

Have you had a heated exchange with someone at work? It's best not to send Reiki to someone who is angry with you. Any kind of energetic exchange will only likely intensify the reaction. Instead, use the Reiki energy to ground yourself, and while giving yourself Reiki, imagine the anger reaction of the other person sliding right past you and not sticking to you. This is more powerful than trying to send Reiki to your boss, for example, which might not be appreciated.

As you sit down to do independent work, whether it be studying, writing, drawing or the like, turn the Reiki energy on with the purpose of clarifying your ability to focus on your work. Use the Reiki as an active study aid.

Before a test or exam, send yourself Reiki with the intention of calming yourself and aiding your memory retention. The energy of Reiki is malleable and can be used for many helpful uses, including some unconventional ones like this.

Are you at a turning point or crossroads in your career? Give yourself an hour with a stack of old magazines. Cut out words and pictures that inspire you, and doodle your own images and text as well. Create a storyboard of the possibilities you envision for a positive future for yourself. Be very specific. Once you've done this, put your picture up in a place you can see it every day and send Reiki to the picture every time you see it.

If you're not such a visual person or you are feeling private about your goals and don't want to post them for everyone in your home to see, make a blessing box. Put in objects that remind you of the larger goals you have for the year ahead. Keep the box on your desk, and send the box Reiki every time you sit down to work. When you have a moment, take out each object and consider how it is manifesting in your life.

Keep a journal specifically geared to noting down your goals. If you are feeling stuck or negative, don't worry. List the negative thoughts that are bothering you in one column, then list their positive counterparts in an adjacent column. You can turn on the Reiki while you formulate the positive thoughts. Rewrite the positive thoughts on a fresh page and send the Reiki to it.

17

Connecting harmonic sound with Reiki

Natural forms have an inner rhythm that can be described by mathematics and geometry. These proportions are also found throughout music. In fact, music is really a sound equivalent of mathematical proportions, and vice versa. These forms and proportions are so innate to the flow of life and they are also very healing for us. They are used in sacred architecture and healing spaces by architects, and the musical sounds can be used in the work of healers as well.

I had the good fortune to study harmonic singing with two great teachers: Ruth Cunningham and Timothy Hill. Here are some suggestions for bringing harmonic sound—that is, sound of sacred proportion—into your work with Reiki. I have modified the exercises to suit my own practice of Reiki and to suit the needs of the students I've worked with over the years, so they are not identical to those taught by Ruth and Timothy.

Hum. Hum anywhere, on the bus, in the shower. Creating a "buzz" in your body generates a sensation that can have a beneficial effect. Humming is a basic vibrational building block that allows us to use sound in our bodies for our own benefit. Thanks go to Ruth Cunningham for the basis of this exercise as well as the one following.

Use specific sounds as you hum, and focus their sound on different parts of your body. Notice where the sounds feel smooth or stick. Allow the vibration of the sound to wash over hurt areas, including areas that feel hurt from emotional wounds. There are traditional yoga sounds associated with each chakra of the body.

Produce a two-tone hum in your body with your own voice, with a simple harmonic singing exercise courtesy of Timothy Hill. Believe it or not, I did this during childbirth and alleviated most of my labor pains during the sounding. Over several breaths, sound out the word "W H Y" and elongate the vowel sounds. Then, do this in reverse, producing the sound "E E Y O W." Listen for the sound of two tones resonating in your own ears. It is sometimes easier to hear the harmonic tones of another person before yourself. With a group, you can sing all these notes simultaneously to create a healing effect.

Create a percussive sound using clapping, clicking, tapping or drumming. This can have a dramatic effect on a person or in a space as old emotional and physical patterns shift.

Use instruments known to produce a soothing harmonic tone effect. This might be a Tibetan singing bowl, harmonic crystal bowl, tuning fork or bell.

In many traditions the instruments mentioned are considered to be sacred, so please regard them as such in your practice. These instruments can be incorporated into a Reiki session or an energetic space clearing session.

Use the power of song or chant. If you practice in a tradition rich in songs or chants, these can be incorporated into your healing practices. I encourage you to explore the songs and chants of cultures outside your own as they can be tremendously illuminating. Treat these vehicles of music as sacred, as they generally are in their root traditions.

If you are simply not at all inclined to produce sounds—not feeling musical today or shy—put on some recorded music that makes you feel expanded and well and relaxed.

18

Setting up your Reiki practice

As we have discussed, Reiki can be incorporated into your own work life or it can be a stand-alone practice in which you see private Reiki clients. If you choose to create a Reiki business, first you need to practice. I recommend that you pursue your studies in Reiki to develop your power of healing, before you begin to offer this as a service. You can teach Reiki once you have become a certified Reiki Master Teacher.

Here are some considerations.

Participate in Reiki shares and Reiki circles. These are local gatherings of Reiki practitioners who wish to keep up their skills and sometimes attract people with no Reiki skills but who wish to receive a brief healing treatment. Sessions are usually ten to fifteen minutes and in a group setting. It is common to offer a small donation to the host of the share, to cover the cost of snacks, etcetera.

Please verify your regional requirements for licensing, insurance and registration. Check in with federal, state, provincial and county-level regulations as they can change. There are a variety of voluntary professional organizations for Reiki practitioners around the world. Find out more about those in your home country and region.

You can work out of your house or out of a studio. Either way, consider purchasing a basic liability insurance policy. Again, check your local zoning ordinance for restrictions.

Consider the comfort of you and your clients. Purchase a good quality massage or Reiki table. These can be found at many sites on the internet.

The shared wisdom among Reiki practitioners is that there is always enough business to go around. Other practitioners have clients who are attracted to them, and you will have clients who are attracted to you. Reiki is all about energy flow and you will magnetize the people who you are to work with.

There are no set fees for Reiki treatments. Do some research about the going rates in your area. Some people feel they ought not charge for a service like Reiki. While it is true that you cannot put a price on the subtle flow of energy, it is also true that your time and expertise are valuable and worth compensation. You can have adjustable rates and offer pro bono (free) services to some if that feels right to you.

Advertise your availability as a practitioner. Visualize a full and fulfilling practice with the right clients for you.

19

Continuing studies in Reiki

Depending upon the Reiki lineage you come through, there are different ways of pursuing the study and practice of Reiki. In the stream of Usui Reiki I teach, there are four levels of instruction:

Level 1 (for self-healing and healing others);

Level 2 (healing with the additional use of three symbols);

Advanced Reiki Training or ART (healing with the master symbol);

Reiki Master Training (learning to teach others Reiki).

With every additional level, your capacity to channel Reiki energy increases. You can think of yourself like a pipe of widening diameter, able to hold a greater flow with each added level. Some teachers say that the capacity to channel does not change, but that the incremental levels are separated so that the practitioner's own healing can amplify at a comfortable rate.

There is often a separation of two months between Levels 1 and 2, and a separation of one year between Level 2 and the Advanced Reiki Training (ART). ART and Master training are often taught in the same week.

Practice time is essential throughout. It is up to the individual student in consultation with their teacher to decide the appropriate spacing of Reiki training sessions. In some cases, as in the Balkans during the last war, Reiki was taught from Level 1 right through to Reiki Master Training over the course of one weekend, because that was what was appropriate for the healing needs of the people and place and time.[1]

You can be attuned at each level as many times as you wish. Additional attunements will act like a super-charged Reiki session and will introduce new lineages that trace back to Usui, thereby rounding out your skills as a Reiki practitioner.

[1] Reiki in the Balkans: (Chowdhury, 2007)

20

Using symbols: a higher level of study

If you continue with studies in Reiki, you will encounter Reiki symbols. Traditionally, Reiki symbols are kept private and shown only between teacher and student. This is no longer the case with ease of internet sharing, and yet, I will endeavor to keep to the tradition while recognizing that most of you will have an opportunity to view the Reiki symbols outside of a traditional teaching environment. I don't personally have a strong opinion on this subject; since some others do, I will maintain the tradition.

My experience with the symbols is a powerful one. Symbols become a focus for intention, and it is not any different within the practice and tradition of Reiki. By focusing one's intention on the symbols, one taps into and amplifies one's own ability to channel the energy. That's really all there is to it, in my eyes. It's a bit of a mind game if you like, literally: you're focusing your mind with intent. And that makes you a more powerful focuser, or allower, of energy flow. Nothing particularly magical about it, just logical to me.

So, if you are interested in higher

studies in Reiki, seek a teacher who enhances your sense of focus and with whom you feel well-aligned. And then you'll tap into the power of the symbols quite naturally after that.

21

A Reiki blessing by Mildred McCaine, in closing

I had a great deal of fun writing a character in my novel, Mildred McCaine, who is a Reiki Master. She's a light-hearted person and you can read more about her in *The Erenwine Agenda*. She's also one of the key figures in *Otter Coast*, still in development as of this writing. This is a Reiki blessing from Mildred, in the context of *The Erenwine Agenda* story:

"You two need some Reiki to calm you down." Mildred closed her eyes, paused for a moment, then came forward and put a hand on the top of each of their heads. "I ask that the clear stream of Reiki be passed through me in a blessing for these two in their journey of understanding together, and that they be able to move forward without holding up the rest of us." She snorted a laugh and withdrew her hands. "That ought to work."

22

Resources about Reiki

Adam, *The Path of the Dreamhealer: My Journey Through the Miraculous World of Energy Healing*, New York: Penguin Group, 2007.

"Alternative and Complementary Therapies", United States Department of Veterans Affairs, February 2007, http://www.ptsd.va.gov/public/pages/treatment-ptsd.asp

Chowdhury, Cassandra, Personal Correspondence with Usui Reiki Master Teacher, 2007.

Clow, Barbara Hand, *Alchemy of the Nine Dimensions*, Charlottesville: Hampton Roads Publishing Company, Inc., 2004.

"Complementary and Alternative Medicine at the War Related Illness and Injury Study Center", *WRIISC Advantage: A National Newsletter for Veterans and their Health Care Providers*, US Department of Veterans Affairs, September 2009, http://www.warrelatedillness.va.gov/docs/newsletter/Tri-WRIISC-newsletter-September-2009.pdf

Dale, Cyndi, *The Subtle Body: An Encyclopedia of Your Energetic Anatomy*, Boulder: Sounds True, Inc., 2009.

Doi, Hiroshi, *Modern Reiki Method for Healing*, Coquitlam: Fraser Journal Publishing, 2000.

Ellyard, Lawrence, *Reiki: 200 Questions and Answers for Beginners*, Ropley: John Hunt Publishing Ltd., 2006.

Fernandez, Carmen, *Reiki: How to Channel the Power of Universal Love and Healing*, London: Anness Publishing Ltd., 2004.

Lübeck, Walter, *The Chakra Energy Cards: Healing Words for Body, Mind and Soul for all Forms of Energy Healing and Reiki Treatments*, Twin Lakes: Lotus Press, 2003.

Macrae, Janet, *Therapeutic Touch: A Practical Guide*, New York: Alfred A. Knopf, 2007.

OMA Group and Avery, Frankie Z., *Handbook for Healers: Guidelines for a Wellness Practice*, Flagstaff: Light Technology, 2009.

Oschman, James L, Interviewed by Rand, William Lee, "Science and the Human Energy Field," in Reiki News Magazine, Vol. 1, Issue 3, Winter 2002.

Rand, William Lee, *Reiki: The Healing Touch, First and Second Degree Manual Including Japanese Reiki Techniques and Hayashi Healing Guide*, Southfield: Vision Publications, 2000.

"Reiki", American Cancer Society, November 2008, http://www.cancer.org/docroot/ETO/content/ETO_5_3X_Reiki.asp?sitearea=ETO

"Reiki: An Introduction", NIH (National Institutes of Health), NCCAM (National Center for Complementary and Alternative Medicine), US Department of Health and Human Services, July 2008, http://nccam.nih.gov/health/reiki/D315_BKG.pdf

Riazat Butt, "Catholic Bishops in US Ban Japanese Reiki" in *The Guardian*, http://www.guardian.co.uk/world/2009/mar/31/us-catholic-bishops-reiki

Roberts, Llyn and Levy, Robert, *Shamanic Reiki: Expanded Ways of Working with Universal Life Force Energy*, Ropley: O Books, 2008.

Tenzin Wangyal Rinpoche, *Healing with Form, Energy and Light: The Five Elements in Tibetan Shamanism, Tantra and Dzogchen*, Ithaca: Snow Lion Publications, 2002.

"Therapeutic Touch – History and Philosophy", Beth Israel Hospital Continuum Center for Health and Healing, New York, March 2003, http://www.healthandhealingny.org/complement/therap_history.asp

Usui, Mikao and Petter, Frank Arjava, *The Original Reiki Handbook of Dr.*

Mikao Usui, Twin Lakes: Lotus Press, 2000.

www.ingramcontent.com/pod-product-compliance
Lightning Source LLC
Chambersburg PA
CBHW070435010526
44118CB00014B/2050